Francis Frith's
Northamptonshire

Photographic Memories

Francis Frith's
Northamptonshire

Nick Channer

First published in the United Kingdom in 2001 by
Frith Book Company Ltd

Hardback Edition 2001
ISBN 1-85937-150-7

Reprinted in Paperback 2005
ISBN 1-84589-074-4

British Library Cataloguing in Publication Data

Francis Frith's Northamptonshire
Nick Channer

Frith Book Company Ltd
Frith's Barn, Teffont,
Salisbury, Wiltshire SP3 5QP
Tel: +44 (0) 1722 716 376
Email: info@francisfrith.co.uk
www.francisfrith.co.uk

Printed and bound in Great Britain

Front Cover: Kettering, Gold Street 1922 72231

The colour-tinting is for illustrative purposes only, and is not intended to be historically accurate

AS WITH ANY HISTORICAL DATABASE THE FRITH ARCHIVE IS CONSTANTLY BEING CORRECTED AND IMPROVED
AND THE PUBLISHERS WOULD WELCOME INFORMATION ON OMISSIONS OR INACCURACIES

Contents

Francis Frith: *Victorian Pioneer*

FRANCIS FRITH, Victorian founder of the world-famous photographic archive, was a complex and multi-talented man. A devout Quaker and a highly successful Victorian businessman, he was both philosophical by nature and pioneering in outlook.

By 1855 Francis Frith had already established a wholesale grocery business in Liverpool, and sold it for the astonishing sum of £200,000, which is the equivalent today of over £15,000,000. Now a very rich man, he was able to indulge his passion for travel. As a child he had pored over travel books written by early explorers, and his fancy and imagination had been stirred by family holidays to the sublime mountain regions of Wales and Scotland. 'What lands of spirit-stirring and enriching scenes and places!' he had written. He was to return to these scenes of grandeur in later years to 'recapture the thousands of vivid and tender memories', but with a different purpose. Now in his thirties, and captivated by the new science of photography, Frith set out on a series of pioneering journeys to the Nile regions that occupied him from 1856 until 1860.

Intrigue and Adventure

He took with him on his travels a specially-designed wicker carriage that acted as both dark-room and sleeping chamber. These far-flung journeys were packed with intrigue and adventure. In his life story, written when he was sixty-three, Frith tells of being held captive by bandits, and of fighting 'an awful midnight battle to the very point of surrender with a deadly pack of hungry, wild dogs'. Sporting flowing Arab costume, Frith arrived at Akaba by camel sixty years before Lawrence, where he encountered 'desert princes and rival sheikhs, blazing with jewel-hilted swords'.

During these extraordinary adventures he was assiduously exploring the desert regions bordering the Nile and patiently recording the antiquities and peoples with his camera. He was the first photographer to venture beyond the sixth cataract. Africa was still the mysterious 'Dark Continent', and Stanley and Livingstone's historic meeting was a decade into the future. The conditions for picture taking confound belief. He laboured for hours in his wicker dark-room in the sweltering heat of the desert, while the volatile chemicals fizzed dangerously in their trays. Often he was forced to work in remote tombs and caves where conditions were cooler. Back in London he exhibited his photographs and was 'rapturously cheered' by members of the Royal Society. His reputation as a

photographer was made overnight. An eminent modern historian has likened their impact on the population of the time to that on our own generation of the first photographs taken on the surface of the moon.

Venture of a Life-Time

Characteristically, Frith quickly spotted the opportunity to create a new business as a specialist publisher of photographs. He lived in an era of immense and sometimes violent change. For the poor in the early part of Victoria's reign work was a drudge and the hours long, and people had precious little free time to enjoy themselves. Most had no transport other than a cart or gig at their disposal, and had not travelled far beyond the boundaries of their own town or village. However,

by the 1870s, the railways had threaded their way across the country, and Bank Holidays and half-day Saturdays had been made obligatory by Act of Parliament. All of a sudden the ordinary working man and his family were able to enjoy days out and see a little more of the world.

With characteristic business acumen, Francis Frith foresaw that these new tourists would enjoy having souvenirs to commemorate their days out. In 1860 he married Mary Ann Rosling and set out with the intention of photographing every city, town and village in Britain. For the next thirty years he travelled the country by train and by pony and trap, producing fine photographs of seaside resorts and beauty spots that were keenly bought by millions of Victorians. These prints were painstakingly pasted into family albums and pored over during the dark nights of winter, rekindling precious memories of summer excursions.

The Rise of Frith & Co

Frith's studio was soon supplying retail shops all over the country. To meet the demand he gathered about him a small team of photographers, and published the work of independent artist-photographers of the calibre of Roger Fenton and Francis Bedford. In order to gain some understanding of the scale of Frith's business one only has to look at the catalogue issued by Frith & Co in 1886: it runs to some 670 pages, listing not only many thousands of views of the British Isles but also many photographs of most European countries, and China, Japan, the USA and Canada – note the sample page shown on page 9 from the hand-written *Frith & Co* ledgers detailing pictures taken. By 1890 Frith had created the greatest specialist photographic publishing company in the

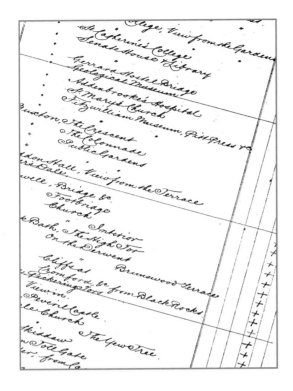

Frith's death, a new card measuring 5.5 x 3.5 inches became the standard format, but it was not until 1902 that the divided back came into being, with address and message on one face and a full-size illustration on the other. *Frith & Co* were in the vanguard of postcard development, and Frith's sons Eustace and Cyril continued their father's monumental task, expanding the number of views offered to the public and recording more and more places in Britain, as the coasts and countryside were opened up to mass travel.

Francis Frith died in 1898 at his villa in Cannes, his great project still growing. The archive he created continued in business for another seventy years. By 1970 it contained over a third of a million pictures of 7,000 cities, towns and villages. The massive photographic record Frith has left to us stands as a living monument to a special and very remarkable man.

world, with over 2,000 outlets – more than the combined number that Boots and WH Smith have today! The picture on the right shows the *Frith & Co* display board at Ingleton in the Yorkshire Dales (left of window). Beautifully constructed with a mahogany frame and gilt inserts, it could display up to a dozen local scenes.

Postcard Bonanza

The ever-popular holiday postcard we know today took many years to develop. In 1870 the Post Office issued the first plain cards, with a pre-printed stamp on one face. In 1894 they allowed other publishers' cards to be sent through the mail with an attached adhesive halfpenny stamp. Demand grew rapidly, and in 1895 a new size of postcard was permitted called the court card, but there was little room for illustration. In 1899, a year after

Frith's Archive: *A Unique Legacy*

FRANCIS FRITH'S legacy to us today is of immense significance and value, for the magnificent archive of evocative photographs he created provides a unique record of change in 7,000 cities, towns and villages throughout Britain over a century and more. Frith and his fellow studio photographers revisited locations many times down the years to update their views, compiling for us an enthralling and colourful pageant of British life and character.

We tend to think of Frith's sepia views of Britain as nostalgic, for most of us use them to conjure up memories of places in our own lives with which we have family associations. It often makes us forget that to Francis Frith they were records of daily life as it was actually being lived in the cities, towns and villages of his day. The Victorian age was one of great and often bewildering change for ordinary people, and though the pictures evoke an impression of slower times, life was as busy and hectic as it is today.

We are fortunate that Frith was a photographer of the people, dedicated to recording the minutiae of everyday life. For it is this sheer wealth of visual data, the painstaking chronicle of changes in dress, transport, street layouts, buildings, housing, engineering and landscape that captivates us so much today. His remarkable images offer us a powerful link with the past and with the lives of our ancestors.

Today's Technology

Computers have now made it possible for Frith's many thousands of images to be accessed almost instantly. In the Frith archive today, each photograph is carefully 'digitised' then stored on a CD Rom. Frith archivists can locate a single photograph amongst thousands within seconds. Views can be catalogued and sorted under a variety of categories of place and content to the immediate benefit of researchers.

Inexpensive reference prints can be created for them at the touch of a mouse button, and a wide range of books and other printed materials assembled and published for a wider, more general readership - in the next twelve months over a hundred Frith local history titles will be published! The day-to-day workings of the archive are very different from how they were in Francis Frith's time: imagine the herculean task of sorting through eleven tons of glass negatives as Frith had to do to locate a particular sequence of pictures! Yet

THE FRANCIS FRITH COL
Photographic publishers since

HOME | PHOTO SEARCH | BOOKS | PORTFOLIO | GALLERY
Products | History | Other Collections | Contact us | Help?

your town, your village

365,000 photographs of 7,000 towns and villages, taken between 1860 & 1970.

The Frith Archive
The Frith Archive is the remarkable legacy of its energetic and visionary founder. Today, the Frith archive is the only nationally important archive of its kind still in private ownership.

The Collection is world-renowned for the extraordinary quality of its images.

The Gallery
This month The Frith Gallery features images from "Frith's Egypt".

News...
Image update complete.
An additional 5,000 images have been added and the quality of all images has now been improved.

Sample Chapters avaliable.
The first selection of sample chapters from the Frith Book Co.'s extensive range is now available. All are offered in Pdf format for easy downloading and viewing.

See Frith at www.francisfrith.co.uk

the archive still prides itself on maintaining the same high standards of excellence laid down by Francis Frith, including the painstaking cataloguing and indexing of every view.

It is curious to reflect on how the internet now allows researchers in America and elsewhere greater instant access to the archive than Frith himself ever enjoyed. Many thousands of individual views can be called up on screen within seconds on one of the Frith internet sites, enabling people living continents away to revisit the streets of their ancestral home town, or view places in Britain where they have enjoyed holidays. Many overseas researchers welcome the chance to view special theme selections, such as transport, sports, costume and ancient monuments.

We are certain that Francis Frith would have heartily approved of these modern developments in imaging techniques, for he himself was always working at the very limits of Victorian photographic technology.

The Value of the Archive Today

Because of the benefits brought by the computer, Frith's images are increasingly studied by social historians, by researchers into genealogy and ancestory, by architects, town planners, and by teachers and schoolchildren involved in local history projects.

In addition, the archive offers every one of us an opportunity to examine the places where we and our families have lived and worked down the years. Highly successful in Frith's own era, the archive is now, a century and more on, entering a new phase of popularity.

The Past in Tune with the Future

Historians consider the Francis Frith Collection to be of prime national importance. It is the only archive of its kind remaining in private ownership and has been valued at a million pounds. However, this figure is now rapidly increasing as digital technology enables more and more people around the world to enjoy its benefits.

Francis Frith's archive is now housed in an historic timber barn in the beautiful village of Teffont in Wiltshire. Its founder would not recognize the archive office as it is today. In place of the many thousands of dusty boxes containing glass plate negatives and an all-pervading odour of photographic chemicals, there are now ranks of computer screens. He would be amazed to watch his images travelling round the world at unimaginable speeds through network and internet lines.

The archive's future is both bright and exciting. Francis Frith, with his unshakeable belief in making photographs available to the greatest number of people, would undoubtedly approve of what is being done today with his lifetime's work. His photographs, depicting our shared past, are now bringing pleasure and enlightenment to millions around the world a century and more after his death.

Northamptonshire - *An Introduction*

A COUNTY OF TALL church spires and quaint ironstone cottages, Northamptonshire lies at the heart of England. It has been described as bland and uninspiring by those who fail to appreciate its delicate beauty and sense of history: on the surface it may appear to be a typical English shire, but look more closely and explore its back roads and byways - you will find a wealth of riches to discredit its harshest critics.

Standing in the shadow of neighbouring Warwickshire and Oxfordshire, and often dubbed the county of spires and squires, Northamptonshire covers almost 1,000 square miles of fertile English countryside. Stretching from Buckinghamshire and Bedfordshire in the south to Leicestershire and Lincolnshire in the north, its roots lie deep in the past, in a world far removed from the present day.

Our island history was written here, when Cavaliers charged recklessly across these fields and blood flowed down the lanes in a swollen stream at the Battle of Naseby.

For 2,000 years Northamptonshire has witnessed some of the great events that have helped to shape our past. Roman legions came this way during the Roman occupation, marching northwards along Watling Street, and later the Saxons made their way here from the south. The county's sprawling forests were the favoured hunting grounds of the Danes and Normans, and here the Council met to enforce the Constitutions of Clarendon, drawn up in Wiltshire to regulate and monitor the conduct of the clergy.

It was here in central England, too, that the Magna Carta barons met, and it was through

Northamptonshire that Edward I travelled at the end of the 13th century, performing the sad task of escorting his wife Eleanor's body from Lincoln to Westminster Abbey. The funeral cortege stopped twice in the county; Edward later marked the route of his journey with a series of ornate crosses. More than 700 years later, at the close of the 20th century, Northamptonshire once more was etched into the pages of history when Diana, Princess of Wales, watched by millions throughout the world, made her final journey home to Althorp, where she was buried in private in the grounds of the great house.

The beautiful but ill-fated Mary, Queen of Scots, one of our most famous monarchs, spent her last days in Northamptonshire, detained at Fotheringhay Castle near Oundle. The fugitive Queen was kept in what was described as 'honourable custody'; for nearly 20 years she was transferred from castle to castle while Queen Elizabeth I decided what to do with her. While imprisoned, Mary became involved in a secret conspiracy to assassinate Queen Elizabeth and thereby secure her place on the throne. The plot was uncovered, and Mary was subsequently put on trial for treason. On 14 October 1586, in the hall of Fotheringhay Castle, the trial began. Mary defended herself skilfully, but to no avail. Her English judges decreed her guilty. Four months later, in February 1587, Mary Queen of Scots dressed herself for the last time in her state robes. She walked firmly into the hall of the castle where the black-clad executioners waited, showing no outward signs of fear. 'I forgive you with all my heart', she told them as they knelt before her. Moments later it was over. The Scottish Queen was dead.

Northamptonshire's tenuous link with George Washington has long attracted American tourists. Sulgrave Manor came into the possession of the Washington family at the Dissolution of the Monasteries when Lawrence Washington, twice mayor of Northampton, from whom George Washington was directly descended, bought it from Henry VIII. It was he who built Sulgrave Manor, which remained in the family until 1610.

Northamptonshire's churches also play a key role in shaping the county's character. There is a strong Saxon influence here, and the legacy of the Norman builders is evident too. The striking architectural heritage of the 13th century is best appreciated in the churches of Warmington, Brington, Oundle and Higham Ferrers, while the splendid Perpendicular style can be seen at Fotheringhay, Ashby St Ledgers, Easton Neston, Charwelton and Kettering.

But it is not just churches for which Northamptonshire is justly famous. There is no better building material than limestone, and when iron has added a hint of colour to warm the stone the effect gladdens the eye. Many small towns and villages in the county make good use of these building materials: if you embark on a leisurely tour through Northamptonshire, you will see the

ironstone influence is evident virtually everywhere you go.

Many of the photographs in this book depict typical village scenes where the warmth of ironstone is clearly apparent. The towns of Northampton, Oundle, Wellingborough, Daventry, Brackley and Kettering are also featured; when they were photographed, boot- and shoe-making were the main industries within the county boundary. The growth in footwear manufacture was influenced by two natural factors - lush grasslands and extensive forests. The bark of oak trees provided the tanning materials, and the flocks and herds grazing on the grassland the hides for the leather.

Francis Frith and his team of photographers were fortunate not to omit Northamptonshire on their travels. The county photographs well, and they carefully ensured that a wide variety of subjects was captured for posterity. Most of the pictures were taken before I was born, yet they serve to remind us of times past that we can all remember, providing a fascinating insight into the daily pattern of our lives,

in both town and country. Much has changed in our modern world, and yet much reassuringly stays the same. Visit some of the places photographed, and compare the image in the book with the reality of today. Frith's revealing portraits of towns, villages and rural scenes provide an endless source of fascination.

If you lived through the 1950s, many of these pictures will stir memories of shopping trips to town, visits to country churches and excursions to pretty villages. They remind us, too, how fashions have changed, how much traffic has increased over the years and how bustling town centres have made room for dazzling new shopping complexes. We may not always want to be reminded of so much change, but we cannot escape it. Apart from evoking memories of distant decades, Frith's photographs create a permanent social record for our children and grandchildren to study and learn from in the years ahead. These fascinating pictures of 20th-century Northamptonshire represent unique images that will never fade.

Around Brackley

Aynho
Brackley Road c1955 A299003
Standing on a hilltop, Aynho is Northamptonshire's most southerly village, and one of its most picturesque. These pretty thatched cottages are among many charming buildings of great character to be found here. Many of the houses in the old part of Aynho are built of local limestone, and most were originally thatched.

▼ Towcester, Market Place and the Town Hall c1955 T105008
Towcester is a small old town on the Tove, with a number of Georgian houses and a pleasant market place. At the far end of the market place stands the imposing Victorian Town Hall, while on the right of the picture is a sign for the historic 15th-century Talbot Hotel. The Romans built the walled town of Lactodorum here.

▼ Brackley, Market Place c1950 B698007
Until the latter part of the 20th century, the quaint stone-built town of Brackley suffered from increasing congestion. A bypass was eventually constructed, and the A43 was diverted away from the town centre. Today, an air of calm pervades the streets of Brackley, much as it did in the mid 1950s when this picture was taken.

**▲ Brackley
The Town Hall c1950**
B698010
A horse-drawn cart carrying sacks makes its way up alongside Brackley's early 18th-century Town Hall, which was built for the Duke of Bridgewater and is attributed to Wren. Note the high roof and cupola. Once an important wool centre, Brackley is a pleasant country town; its wide main street is more than a mile long.

◄ **Upper Boddington The Village c1960** U51001
Close to the Warwickshire county boundary and its near neighbour Lower Boddington, Upper Boddington has changed a good deal since this photograph was taken. New houses have sprung up in the village, and older properties have been restored; yet it remains a very pleasant community. The parish of Boddington is recorded in the Domesday Book as Botendon.

Around Daventry

Braunston, The Canal c1965 B778016
The village of Braunston lies on a hill overlooking a picturesque stretch of the Grand Union Canal, one of Britain's most famous inland waterways. Near here is a long tunnel through which boatmen once manoeuvred their narrow boats by exercising maximum physical effort. They lay on their backs and pushed with their feet against the tunnel roof.

Byfield, High Street c1955 B703002
This photograph of the village of Byfield, on the old turnpike road midway between Daventry and Banbury, shows plenty of pedestrians, but no traffic. On the right is Adams, the family grocer, and further down is the Rose and Crown. The village once had its own railway station and iron workings, as well as a farm with nine dairy herds.

Braunston, High Street
c1950 B778004

An interesting mix of architectural styles characterises Braunston's High Street. Some of the houses are built of brick, some of stone. The van parked on the left of the street is advertising Mackeson's stout. Television was still in its infancy in the mid 1950s, so there were few aerials to be seen in those days.

▼ Lilbourne, The Green
c1955 L442004

This is a classic English village setting, with rows of cottages overlooking a green and an old red telephone box. The old black and white signpost points to nearby Watling Street, one of Britain's most famous Roman roads and now the A5. The M1 is also close by, though it had not been built when this photograph was taken.

◄ Lilbourne
The Church c1955
L442002

In a field near Lilbourne's All Saints church are the remains of several burial mounds from the Roman encampment. The church, noted for its low battlemented 15th-century tower, dates back to the 13th and 14th centuries. The village's close proximity to Watling Street made it a prosperous community in medieval times.

Naseby, The Monument c1955 ▶
N200001

Naseby is famous for its Civil War battle of 1645 between King Charles I and the Parliamentarians, with Sir Thomas Fairfax as Commander-in-Chief and Oliver Cromwell as Lieutenant-General of the Horse. More than likely, Cromwell stabled his horses in the church. The monument in the picture is one of two such memorials which recall a significant event in Naseby's history.

▼ Welton, The Village c1955
W477004

North of Daventry and close to the border with Warwickshire, Welton stands on a hillside above the Grand Union Canal. Its name comes from the springs and wells in the area. The White Horse pub can just be seen on the right, and on the left by the school sign are familiar adverts for Lyons Ice Cream and Lyons Tea.

▲ Welton, The Village c1955 W477005

Down the street stands Welton's church, dedicated to St Martin and distinguished by its square 14th-century tower. Inside is an ancient tub-shaped font, said to be Saxon. A small brass recalls that in 1899 five sons of the village carved the splendid pulpit 'for the love of the church'. They were also responsible for the alms box, which represents an open hand appealing for coins.

◄ Woodford Halse School Street c1965

W552014

Before the dawn of the railway era, Woodford Halse was a sleepy community untouched by time. With the cutting of the Great Central line through the Midlands towards the end of the last century, the place changed almost beyond recognition. Around the time this photograph was taken, the village station and the line were axed, and a stillness descended on Woodford Halse once more.

▼ **Yelvertoft, Tanney Lane c1955** Y44001
Yelvertoft stands near the Grand Union Canal, on a stream which flows into the Avon. The village side streets are reminders of local farmers who long ago made their living off the land here. In the early part of the 20th century the nearby wharf was still a bustling place.

▼ **Yelvertoft, The Post Office and Main Road c1955** Y44012
In the days when the English village was a thriving community, Yelvertoft benefited from two bakers, a butcher, a blacksmith, three inns and a grocer, whose premises can be seen on the left of the main street. Lining the street are various charming cottages and houses of character.

▲ **Weedon Bec
The Village c1955**
W593307
Weedon is split into several settlements. There is Weedon-bec, Upper Weedon and Road Weedon. All of them lie close to Watling Street, the old Roman road which crosses the River Nene in this area.

◄ **Daventry, Market Place c1950** D83008
The cottages on the left of this photograph have all gone now, and in their place is a landscaped public garden area with trees and bushes. The houses on the right of the square remain, and are now whitewashed. The gabled building immediately to the left of the 18th-century parish church, built in the classical style, is an ex-servicemen's club.

▼ **Daventry, The Monument and the Moot Hall c1950** D83003
Dominating this photograph are the tall Moot Hall, now the Daventry Museum and tourist information centre, and the monument, which was erected by members of the National Hunt committee in memory of Edmund Charles Burton - 'a staunch churchman, a renowned sportsman and a man greatly beloved'. The Maple Leaf Court sign, swinging on the street corner, has gone.

▼ **Daventry, High Street c1950** D83002
Stand by the Burton monument and look down the High Street to compare this photograph with the scene today. The Lion and Lamb on the right has changed its name, and is now called Fridays. Lloyds TSB is still there. The road is now narrower with wider pavements.

▲ **Daventry, High Street c1965** D83078
This photograph was taken midway down the High Street. On the extreme right, partly visible, is the entrance to the local Conservative club, and on the left is the facade of the National Provincial Bank, now Nat West. The Co-operative on the right has disappeared; it has been replaced by shop units.

◀ **Daventry, The Recreation Ground c1965** D83085
Children once played on this old railway engine, but today this local landmark is a sad, neglected relic, left over from the great days of steam travel. Fencing now prevents anyone climbing over it for health and safety reasons. The chestnut tree to the right of it has gone, as have most of the houses in the background. A bus station and car park now make up the scene.

Around Oundle

Oundle, Market Place c1950 0103030
Oundle, best known for its public school, lies in
the north-east corner of the county. It may have
expanded somewhat over the years, but it still
remains a compact market town. The Market Place
is still the focal point of Oundle. Note the old-style
telephone box on the right of the photograph.

◄ **Oundle, New Street c1950** 0103029
On the right of the picture is the town war memorial; to the left is the striking grey stone facade of the Talbot Hotel, a gabled 17th-century building. Inside is a splendid Jacobean oak staircase; according to some sources, it comes from nearby Fotheringhay Castle, where Mary Queen of Scots was beheaded in 1587.

◀ Oundle, Market Place c1950 0103033
The Victorian Town Hall in the centre of the Market Place was built by the Watts-Russell family; today it is occupied by local businesses. The Rose & Crown, on the right, is still running, as is the bank next door. The colonnaded building to the right of the inn houses the school bookshop.

▼ Oundle, Benefield Road c1950 0103024
Picturesque stone cottages line Benefield Road. At the far end of the street, dominating the picture, is Jesus Church, built in 1879 by Arthur Blomfield. He also carried out various improvements to Oundle School. The church is now a Roman Catholic one.

◀ Oundle, Stoke Hill c1950 0103026
Jesus Church was designed in the form of a cross, in Gothic style, with tall lancet windows in the nave, chancel and transept. The church has an unusual and distinctive central lantern, which starts as a square and then becomes an octagon, with a dome-shaped ceiling. To the left of the church are the premises of Claridge & Co, grocers.

Oundle, West Street c1950 0103028
With rows of charming buildings and the River Nene flowing on three sides of it, Oundle has often been described as Northamptonshire's most delightful town. This photograph recalls the days when there was very little traffic to clog our town centres. On the right of the picture is a newsagent's window with advertisements for Players cigarettes and Woodbines. Further down the street is a Tate & Lyle delivery van.

◄ **Oundle, West Street c1950** 0103003
West Street includes various almshouses and picturesque stone cottages. The Victoria Inn on the left of the picture is now a private house. Oundle School occupies many buildings in and around the town. The school was founded by William Laxton, a grocer who later became Lord Mayor of London.

▼ **Rockingham
The Village c1960** R353001
Rockingham stands on a steep hill above the River Welland; from the summit you can look out over five counties. Many picturesque thatched cottages and flintstone houses line the street. The village general stores and post office once housed its own manual telephone exchange.

◄ **Rockingham, The Castle c1960** R353009
Above the village of Rockingham lies the splendid castle, built by William the Conqueror on the site of an ancient fortress and at the heart of the great Rockingham Forest. For 500 years it was used as a royal residence and hunting lodge. Charles Dickens stayed at Rockingham Castle, and wrote part of 'Bleak House' here.

Rockingham The Village c1960

R353005

The earliest residence in Rockingham dates from 1670; much of the village was modernised and improved in the 19th century, and then again in the 1950s. Rockingham used to be a market town, but the market ceased long ago. The inn on the left is the Sondes Arms.

Stanion, The Church c1960 S627003

Situated within the remains of the Rockingham Forest, Stanion has thatched and stone-tiled cottages looking towards the graceful tower and spire of its 13th-century church. The steeple is visible from miles away. Inside the church is a bone: according to legend, it is a rib from a cow that provided all the milk for the village!

Corby, Market Square c1965 C337164

Corby was originally a village, but by 1950 its population had increased enormously; during that year it was given New Town status. Many new buildings sprang up in the 1950s and 1960s, including the Civic Centre of 1965 and the Technical Library of 1959. However, it was the unsightly steel works which really put Corby on the map.

Around Kettering

Kettering, The Market 1922 72232
The bank on the left of this photograph became an
insurance office, and the adjoining dental surgery
is also the premises of an insurance company. The
shops and houses to the right of the church have
all gone; now, trees form the boundary. The whole
scene is overlooked by the tower and steeple of
St Peter and St Paul's church.

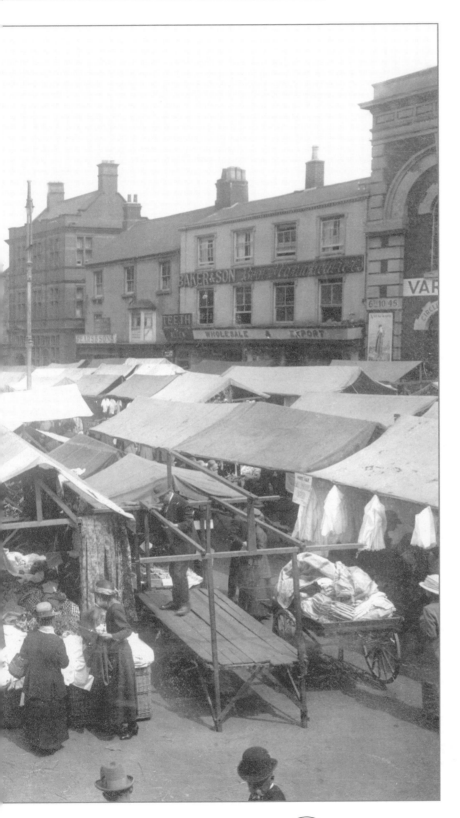

**Kettering
The Market 1922**

72233

This photograph captures the atmosphere and feel of Kettering's bustling market, which is much the same now as it was then. On the extreme right of the picture is the mid 19th-century Corn Exchange. The sign outside reads Circle Gallery - 6-10.45. The building closed some years ago, and is now a branch of Ladbrokes, among other shops.

Kettering, High Street 1922 72228
The Royal Hotel looks pretty much the same today as it did then. Even the AA sign is in the same place, though the current one is a more up-to-date version. One large window also replaces the two to the right of the main entrance.

Kettering, High Street 1922 72227
It's a case of spot the difference here. At first glance this picture looks exactly the same as the other photograph of the Royal Hotel, No 72228, but a closer look reveals subtle changes. A butcher's delivery boy can be seen cycling down the road, more of the shop fronts are covered by awnings, and a uniformed policeman can be seen on the right.

Kettering
High Street 1922 72229
Decorators can be seen at work outside Hepworths. The Pearl
Assurance sign has gone, and the upper windows of this building have
been replaced, but the unusual brick and stone work above them is
still there. The building to the left of it is now a branch of Nat West.

Kettering
High Street c1950 K13023
The old Northamptonshire Union Bank on the right of the picture
is now the Nat West, though fortunately the facade remains intact.
Freeman, Hardy and Willis and the rest of the shops on the left
closed some years ago to make way for modern units. The domed
building, the Old White Horse and the overhead street lighting
have also disappeared.

Kettering, High Street c1950 K13024
Stand in the same spot today and you would not recognise this scene. The Old White Horse has gone, and so
have the buildings on the left. In the distance you can just make out a sign for Bell & Billows, and next to it is an
advertisement which reads: 'New Hoover Electric Washer is here now'.

Kettering, Newland Street 1922 72235
One local resident of Kettering recalls visiting Woodcock's department store on the corner of Newland Street and
Montagu Street as a child in the 1920s and 30s. She and her mother bought ribbons, gloves and socks here, and
the assistant put the money and bill into a brass cylinder which was attached to a wire overhead pulley. The shop
is now an estate agents.

**Kettering
Gold Street 1922**
72231
A Kettering resident
remembers the town
centre in the 1920s and
1930s when policemen,
with arms outstretched,
directed what little
traffic there was,
errand-boys cycled
through the streets
loaded with baskets of
parcels, and horses and
carts clattered between
the buildings. This
photograph captures
the atmosphere of
those far-off days.

Kettering
Gold Street 1922 72230
This photograph shows the junction of Gold Street and Silver
Street. The gabled building on the right with the arches is the Fuller
Baptist Church, named after Andrew Fuller, who founded the
Baptist Missionary Society. All the buildings on the right beyond
the church and many on the left have been replaced. Note the car
and the hats, which are typically 1920s in style.

Kettering, Gold Street c1950 K13042
This picture, taken 30 or so years after photograph No 72230, shows the same buildings you see today. Burtons the tailors is now an estate agents and mortgage shop. Gold Street was a one-way street in the 1950s, with traffic beginning to increase as the motor car became more popular.

Kettering, Montagu Street c1950 K13021
From the junction with Silver Street and Gold Street you can spot the distinctive tall tower of a former boys school, now an educational centre. The building and its tower, distinguished by its tracery and four gables, date back to 1892. The first three shops on the right have all changed hands over the years.

◀ **Kettering
The Art Gallery 1922**
72244
Stand across the road,
roughly in the spot
where this picture was
taken, and you will see
that little has changed,
apart from a few more
trees, some road signs
and plenty of traffic.
The Alfred East Gallery,
opened in 1913 and
named after a local artist,
is distinguished by its
stone walls and Tuscan
columns. To the left
of it is the town library,
opened in 1904.

Kettering, Silver Street c1950 K13018

It would have been necessary to stand in the road to capture this view of Silver Street looking down towards the junction with Gold Street, Newland Street and Montagu Street. The London Grill on the right has gone. The tall building five doors down is a pub, the Rising Sun.

Kettering, The School 1922 72243

This building, next door to the gallery and library, is much the same today as it was in the early 1920s. Built in the Georgian style with a red tiled roof and widely projecting eaves and cornice, the building was originally Kettering High School for girls; it first opened in 1913. The central block includes the old assembly hall.

Thrapston, Chancery Lane c1955 T104002

Thrapston is still remembered for its American connection. Sir John Washington, who was knighted by Charles I and was buried in the local churchyard, was the brother of Lawrence Washington, whose son John emigrated to America and became the great-grandfather of George Washington, the first President of the United States. The church contains a tablet showing the coat of arms from which the Stars and Stripes originate.

▲ **Thrapston, High Street 1951** T104008
Tomlinson's Stores is now the premises of Age Concern, and Goss Bros is now a tea shop. The White Hart
on the right of Thrapston High Street closed in 1970, and was later demolished to make way for a new library
and fire station. Some old stone houses remain, and nearby is a scenic stretch of the River Nene.

◄ **Rushton, The Village c1955** R272009
Rushton is famous in the county for its connection with the Tresham family. They built nearby Rushton Hall. Francis Tresham became one of the Gunpowder Plot conspirators, and approached his uncle Sir Thomas Tresham for financial help. Another notable building associated with this family is Triangular Lodge, an exuberant folly which was designed as an emblem of the Trinity.

◄ Rushton, The Village c1955 R272007

The village of Rushton is mentioned as Riston or Risetone in the Domesday Book. Many of the houses here are built of the familiar ironstone of the oolitic limestone belt, which stretches all the way from South Yorkshire to Dorset. Rushton is a sprawling, scattered community, as this photograph reveals.

▼ Burton Latimer, High Street c1955 B390006

Part of Kettering Borough, Burton Latimer has grown from a farming community into a small town over the years. It was originally associated chiefly with shoe manufacture, though these days its main industries focus on breakfast cereal and aluminium casks for the brewery trade. The Waggon & Horses in the High Street is still in business.

◄ Barton Seagrave, Old Cottages c1955 B700012

Only a couple of miles from Kettering, the village of Barton Seagrave retains plenty of charm and character. These delightful ironstone cottages stand in the lee of the trees; nearby lies Barton Hall, reputed to have been built with stones from a 14th-century castle here. The Hall was constructed during the reign of Queen Elizabeth I. Northamptonshire's most famous historian, John Bridges, was born here in 1666.

▼ Islip, The Village c1950 156001

Situated on high ground on the western bank of the River Nene, between Thrapston and Kettering, Islip is a picturesque village with the buildings in its High Street built mostly of Northamptonshire limestone. Many of the cottages in the village are thatched.

▼ Islip, Country Club House c1950 156004

Once a country club, Islip House was originally the home of Thomas Squire, who was instrumental in making the River Nene navigable between Peterborough and Thrapston. The river was eventually opened to craft in 1737. Initially, wharves were built on both sides of the Nene. Beneath Islip House were bonded wine vaults.

▲ Raunds, High Street c1955 R82017

Midway between Rushden and Thrapston lies the small town of Raunds. In this photograph you can just pick out the spire of the church, soaring 183 feet above the High Street. The top of the spire was struck by lightning in the 19th century and was carefully rebuilt stone by stone.

◄ **Raunds, Brook Street
c1960** R82024
Raunds used to be a
bustling manufacturing
centre for shoes, but
most of the factories have
now gone. Over the years
the town has expanded
considerably; nowadays,
many local inhabitants
commute to work
elsewhere. On the right
of the picture is Barclays
Bank, and next to it is the
National Provincial Bank,
now defunct.

◄ **Desborough
High Street c1965**
D200033
The King's Arms in
Desborough High Street
continues to trade as a
pub, but the New Inn
next to it was demolished
in the 1970s to make
way for the new A6.
Many of the buildings
close to the inn were also
razed to the ground to
accommodate the road.

**◄ Desborough
High Street c1965** D200032
On the road to Market
Harborough, Desborough is
a small town with various
ironstone cottages and inns.
Long ago there was a Saxon
settlement here; three huge
stones were discovered in
the rectory garden, the
largest covered on two sides
with Saxon lettering. A
Saxon mirror and necklace
found here were given to
the British Museum.

**▼ Desborough, The George
Hotel c1960** D200010
Two small boys can be seen
riding along on the
pavement by the George
Hotel. The pub is still there
today, and so is what is
known as the Desborough
Cross to the right of it.
According to some
sources, the cross was
once part of the entrance
to a local country estate.
Further up the street is the
Ritz Cinema, which later
became a ballroom.

**◄ Geddington, The Village
c1955** G84021
Rows of stone cottages
surround the Cross in
Geddington village centre,
built in 1294 to commemorate
Queen Eleanor of Castile, wife
of Edward I. The memorial is
one of 12 original crosses
representing resting places on
the route of her funeral
procession to Westminster
Abbey in 1290. Only three
remain; the other two are at
Hardingstone, near
Northampton, and Waltham
Cross in Hertfordshire. The
cross contains small statues of
the Queen.

Geddington, The Cross c1950 G84010
On the right of the photograph is an advert for Player's, seen all over the country at the time when this picture was taken. Geddington is famous for its May Day tradition of distributing bread throughout the village. In the morning children take flowers to pensioners; then in the afternoon the May Queen is crowned on the steps of the cross.

Geddington, The Village c1955 G84027
Beyond the medieval bridge over the River Ise lies the Church of St Mary Magdalen, distinguished by its tower and octagonal spire. The church received the body of Queen Eleanor overnight before the cortege set off on the next stage of the long journey to London. Nearby there was once a royal hunting palace, though nothing remains of it apart from some fragments in the church.

Geddington
The Village 1922 72253
Contrast and compare this photograph with the 1950s images of
Geddington, and you can see that the village has hardly changed at
all in the intervening years. Various figures can be seen seated by
the 40-ft Cross, which rises from seven steps at the point where
three roads meet.

▼ **Geddington, Boughton House c1955** G84023

Boughton House lies about one and a half miles to the south-east of Geddington. Situated in its own magnificent parkland, the house has been described as the 'English Versailles'. The Duke of Montagu, who lived there, held the post of Ambassador to the Court of Louis XIV, and brought back with him an impressive collection of French furniture and china.

▼ **Rothwell, The Old Town Hall 1922** 72249

Pronounced Rowell, the town quite possibly takes its name from an old Danish word meaning red well. By the Middle Ages it had became a thriving town of some importance. A market charter was granted by King John in 1204. The Market Hall in the town centre was designed by William Grumbald. Work began in 1577, but the building remained unfinished until 1895.

▲ **Rothwell, Market Hill c1955** R322013

The Red Lion Hotel on the right is much the same today. We can glimpse the Market Hall a little beyond it. The shop fronts and buildings on the left are similar to today, but the one major difference is the huge increase in traffic on this road.

◀ **Rothwell, High Street c1955** R322011
This photograph shows the corner of High Street and Bridge Street. The Electricity Service Centre and the London Central Meat Company have been replaced by a beauty salon and a florist. The Old Greyhound Inn is still in business, and the cottages further down still look up the street towards the junction.

▼ **Rothwell, The Church and the Memorial Cross 1922** 72250
The graceful war memorial recalls the men of Rothwell who fought
and died in the Great War. Trees still line the road; at the end of it
stands the town's ironstone Holy Trinity Church, the longest in the
county. The original spire collapsed in the 17th century, but the top
of it has been reset on the stair-turret on the north face of the tower.

▼ **Rothwell, Holy Trinity Church, Bone Crypt c1950** R322016
This gruesome sight still greets visitors today as they descend into the vaulted
13th-century crypt. The crypt was sealed off for years; when it was discovered
by a sexton digging a grave and eventually reopened, it was found to contain
thousands of bones and skulls collected from an old churchyard.

▲ **Rothwell, Market Place
c1950** R322001
The handsome building
on the right with the
flagpole is the Rothwell
branch of the
Conservative Club. Next
to it is the Chequers
Hotel, now a convenience
store. The building is
dated 1734. On the left is
the Market House, and
nearby is the Red Lion.

◀ Rothwell
The Blue Bell Inn c1965
R322055

The Rothwell Industrial Co-operative Society on the right has become the Co-op supermarket, and the Blue Bell is now simply called The Pub. The cottages between the two buildings, further down the street, are now whitewashed. Note the familiar makes of car in this 1960s picture. The road here is much busier today.

▼ Rothwell, Market Place and the Blue Bell Inn c1950 R322002

About ten years before picture No R322055 of the Blue Bell was taken, this view of it was captured through the photographer's lens. The pub, which looks rather drab in this shot, changed its name in 2000. The Woolpack Inn opposite is still trading, and the newsagents on the left-hand side is also still there.

▼ Rothwell, Bridge Street c1950 R322012

The premises of the Rothwell Co-operative Society has changed to an Indian restaurant, and the building to the left of it has gone and been replaced by a chemist's shop. The wall on the left of the picture marks the entrance to the Rothwell House Hotel.

▲ Rothwell, Market Place c1950 R322014

Rothwell's history dates back to long before the Danish invasion of the Dark Ages. 4,000 years ago Bronze Age settlers came to this area, followed by the Romans. Later, when the market charter was granted, King John gave permission for an annual fair which is still held here during the week following Trinity Sunday.

◀ **Rothwell, Market Place c1950** R322005
Rothwell's most famous landmark, the old Market House, is partly visible on the right of this photograph. Around its cornice are Latin inscriptions and 90 coats-of-arms of landed families. The Market House is cross-shaped in plan. Work on the building was finished by J A Gotch, a Northamptonshire architect, who roofed it and filled in the arches.

Around Wellingborough

Bozeat, The Red Lion c1950 B701002
Close to the county boundary with
Buckinghamshire and Bedfordshire, the unusually-
named village of Bozeat was at the heart of a
thriving weaving industry 600 years ago; the
Weavers' Guild donated a rich assortment of gifts
to the church. Later, the village became a centre
for shoe production. In 1914 many soldiers
marched off to war wearing locally-made boots.

▼ **Earls Barton, The Village c1955** E97001

Dominating this photograph is the richly-decorated Saxon tower of the church of All Saints, standing sentinel and soaring above the rooftops of the village. The Earl of Huntingdon lived nearby, and the village gets the other half of its name from his association with barley farming. The Queen Mother has made several visits to Earls Barton.

▼ **Earls Barton, The Village c1955** E97003

Since the 1960s Earls Barton has doubled in size; now the new housing estates in the village attract commuters who travel daily to Northampton, Wellingborough and elsewhere. Earls Barton is surrounded by the lush countryside of the Nene valley, making it popular with house hunters.

▲ **Finedon
The Village c1950**

F18402

Three miles from Wellingborough, between the Nene and the Ise, lies the village of Finedon. Rows of houses and quaint ironstone cottages line the street; in the distance is the familiar figure of the local postman out making his deliveries.

◄ **Finedon, The Village c1950** F18401
Finedon is a large, scattered village with many houses and cottages built by the last squire of the village who tragically lost all three of his sons. On the road to Thrapston is a round tower built by General Arbuthnot, a friend of the Duke of Wellington, to commemorate the Battle of Waterloo.

▼ **Great Doddington, Hard Water Mill c1965** G137011

Hard Water Mill is a noted landmark in this area. Some sources suggest that the Archbishop of Canterbury, Thomas a Becket, fled here after a confrontation with King Henry II at Northampton Castle. The story goes that he was given shelter here by the miller before seeking exile in France. The mill later became a private house.

▼ **Rushden, High Street and the Post Office 1928** R223016

Situated to the south of the Nene valley, Rushden is another of Northamptonshire's footwear manufacturing towns. One local resident recalls a boot and shoe factory which closed down after the First World War when there was no longer any great demand for army boots. Note the imposing Post Office on the left of the street.

▲ **Stanwick, The Village c1960** S628012

Set on a hill above the valley of the Nene, Stanwick lies on the A605. The road sign can be seen pointing to Higham Ferrers. On the left is the edge of the churchyard; beyond it lies Stanwick Post Office, and the premises of the local grocer and draper. Look closely. and you can spot the advertisement for Wall's ice cream.

◀ **Wollaston, High Street c1955** W421013
To the south of Wellingborough lies the village of Wollaston, separated from its neighbour Great Doddington by the River Nene. On the right of the street, on the upper storey, is a sign for Wollaston Band Club. The village still has many pubs and clubs today.

◀ **Irchester, High Street
c1955** 171006
Said to be the largest village
in Northamptonshire,
Irchester now has a
population of more than
5,000. It began as an
agricultural community;
it later developed as an
industrial centre,
concentrating on rush mats,
lace, the quarrying of
ironstone, and the
manufacture of boots and
shoes. Most of the local
industries have now gone.

◄ Wollaston, The Village
c1950 W421001
The Bell Inn displays a prominent sign. One local resident, who was born in 1954, remembers as a girl getting her hair cut here when the inn changed to a hairdresser's. In later years the building was converted to a private house.

▼ Irchester, High Street
c1950 171007
The last building on the right was originally the village bakery and next to it, as seen in this picture, was an off-licence. Peeping into view above the rooftops of these cottages, now sadly gone, is the elegant spire of St Katherine's Church, one of the tallest in the county.

◄ Irchester, High Street
c1950 171008
All the cottages on the right of the street have gone now, and are replaced by modern bungalows and the local library. Some of the buildings on the left have also disappeared over the years. On the left, just out of view, was the old butcher's shop and pie factory.

◀ **Higham Ferrers College Street c1950**
H245002
The jumble of gables and chimneys on the right of the street represents a 17th-century house; opposite it is the entrance to Chichele College, founded by Archbishop Chichele in 1422. The College was built around a quadrangle. It housed twenty members, including eight chaplains, four clerks and six choristers. Henry VIII later dissolved Chichele College, and the buildings were ruinous by the 18th century

◄ Higham Ferrers Market Square c1950

H245011

On the extreme right of the picture is the war memorial, recalling the men of Higham Ferrers who died in both World Wars, and to the left of it, partly screened by trees, is the 13th-century Market Cross. Wedding ceremonies were originally conducted here. The building with the carriage arch on the far left is the Green Dragon Hotel and Restaurant.

◄ Wellingborough, Oxford Street c1955

W279007

A Howe, a ladies and gents' tailor, is now a florist; the coach builders' on the left has been replaced by a modern supermarket. The buildings to the right of it are still there and look much the same. At the end of the row is a pub, the Coach and Horses.

**Wellingborough
Silver Street c1950**

W279005

This photograph was taken at the junction of Silver Street and Oxford Street. The first building on the right is now a cafe, but its overall appearance is much the same. The Angel Hotel on the left closed some years ago, though the prominent lettering on the upper part of the building is still faintly recognisable.

**Wellingborough
Silver Street c1950**
W279008
Many of the shops you
see in this picture have
changed hands. The
shop on the corner with
the awning is now
McDonalds, and what
was United Counties on
the opposite corner is
now a travel shop. The
upper part of the
building looks much the
same today.

Wellingborough, Market Street c1950 W279031
Market Street is now pedestrianised. The Lloyds Bank building on the right has been renovated, though the exterior is similar. The Crown to the right of it is now a building society. The shop next door used to be Green & Valentine, a draper and milliner. Today, this is an office stationers. Modern shops and banks now line both sides of the street. The building with the distinctive dome can still be seen.

Wellingborough, Market Street c1950 W279027
Mentioned in the Domesday Book and briefly a spa town in the 17th century, Wellingborough was granted market rights by King John in 1201. Cromwell stayed here en route to Naseby during the Civil War. The 1928 building on the left of the picture is now an optician's - the date has gone.

Wellingborough
Midland Road c1950 W279025
Note the handsome facade of the Old King's Arms at the top of the
street. The inn is now a carpet shop, though the inn signs above it
remain. The broach spire of Wellingborough parish church peeps
above the rooftops. Inside are stained glass windows by John Piper,
Home and Reyntiens.

**Wellingborough
Midland Road c1950**
W279024
The Granville Hotel on
the extreme left of the
picture closed in the
early 1960s. The
Midland Hotel next door
was demolished and
replaced with an
extension to the town
Post Office, which still
occupies the same site
today. All the buildings
on the right of the
street have gone.

Wellingborough
High Street c1950 W279006
Looking up the High Street from the direction of Silver Street and
Oxford Street shows a quiet street scene with little traffic. Many of
the buildings look much the same, though the road here is much
busier today. The High Street sign is still there, though the shops
below it have changed hands over the years. At the top of the street,
at right angles to the shops, is the United Reformed Church.

Around Northampton

Overstone
Overstone Park c1955 0104020
North-east of Northampton, Overstone is a linear village dating
back to the 18th century. The original village was in front of the
manor house: such was the power and influence of the local
landowner in those days, that the settlement was demolished
and rebuilt outside the park boundary. The public road was also
closed and the grounds landscaped.

◄ **Great Brington The Church 1922**

72215

75 years after this photograph was taken, Great Brington and the adjoining parkland became the focus of world attention when Diana, Princess of Wales was laid to rest in the grounds of Althorp House. Many members of the Spencer family are buried in Great Brington church.

◄ Althorp Park
The House 1922 72211

Althorp dates back to the 16th century. At that time John Spencer, a Warwickshire sheep farmer, acquired the estate and created a park of some 300 acres here. Building work began in 1573, in the reign of Elizabeth I, and the house has been the home of the Spencer family ever since.

▼ Great Brington
The Post Office 1922

72214

Here we see Great Brington's picturesque stone and thatched cottages. The village Post Office on the right has a small sign attached to the wall which reads 'Post Office for money orders, savings bank, parcel post, telegraph, insurance and annuity business'. The Post Office is part of the Althorp Estate.

◄ Blisworth
The Canal c1955

B283391

This impressive picture captures a charming rural scene. In the foreground is the Grand Union Canal, with the houses of Blisworth and the 15th-century tower of the church to be seen on the opposite bank. During the 18th century, Blisworth was the venue for loading and unloading boats from London, the Midlands and the North.

◀ **Castle Ashby 1922**
72221
This magnificent house is situated in grounds landscaped by Capability Brown. Its avenues were planted following a visit by William III. The house was started by the 1st Lord Compton, later the Earl of Northampton, in 1574. Look closely, and you will see that the parapet along the top balustrade has a carved Latin inscription.

Blisworth, The Village c1955 B283001

Phipps ales and stout and wines and spirits can just be seen advertised on either side of the main door of the thatched Royal Oak in Blisworth. On the corner by the wall is a Midland bus timetable; across the road is Blisworth Post Office, with its huge advert for Players Navy Mixture.

▼ Hardingstone The Green c1965 H418302

Like Geddington, the village of Hardingstone is famous for its Queen Eleanor Cross, erected by Edward I in memory of his wife. The funeral procession rested here en route to London in 1290. Originally the village extended no further than Back Lane, Coldstream Lane, the High Street and the houses in the vicinity of the green, which we see in this photograph.

◀ Great Houghton High Street c1965 G223007

Modern 1950s and 1960s houses of various different styles can be seen on the right of Great Houghton High Street in this photograph. Great Houghton is only a couple of miles from the centre of Northampton, on the southern slopes of the Nene valley.

▼ **Great Houghton, The Old Cherry Tree Inn c1965** G223005

The Old Cherry Tree Inn, one of two pubs in Great Houghton, is a cosy village hostelry with quaint beams and plenty of character. A cherry tree is depicted on the inn sign, and on the outside wall is the date 1576 - the year the pub was built. There are no fruit machines inside, and little has changed in the bar over the years.

▼ **Creaton, The Village c1965** C577008

Located about eight miles north-west of Northampton, the village of Creaton used to comprise two communities - Great Creaton and Little Creaton. It may look like a peaceful and unremarkable village where little happens, but this community has a tenuous link with the American political system. The great-great grandmother of George Washington was born in the area.

▲ **Duston, Main Road c1960** D202008

A mile or two to the west of Northampton, the village of Duston is steeped in history. Over 12,000 pieces of worked flints including arrow-heads, scrapers, saws, borers and hammers were discovered here, indicating the existence of a New Stone Age settlement in the area. This photograph shows the village centre with its rows of pretty cottages.

Milton Malsor, The Post Office c1960 M294006
Milton Malsor is a charming, typically English village to the south of Northampton and the M1. This picture shows the village post office, delightfully housed in a picturesque thatched cottage. Most of Milton Malsor's buildings date from the 17th and 18th centuries. Opposite the post office is a classic Morris estate car, a familiar sight in the 1950s and 60s.

◀ **Moulton, High Street c1950** M295007
Despite its close proximity to Northampton, the heart of Moulton remains a conservation area. On the left of the picture are the premises of the Central Garage; its logo can also be seen adorning the side of the van parked on the street corner. On the opposite pavement is a pram, a rare sight nowadays.

◄ **Moulton, West Street c1950** M295001

Moulton is only a stone's throw from the centre of Northampton; when the town thrived on shoe manufacture, many men and women walked from this village to work in the shoe factories. On the left in this picture are the premises of a high class boot and shoe repairer. Note the advert for Cherry Blossom.

▼ **Yardley Hastings Little Street c1950** Y43005

There are plenty of thatched cottages in Yardley Hastings, a pretty village on the A428 between Northampton and Bedford. About fifteen years before this picture was taken, in October 1940, a German parachutist was discovered and captured by two local men. When questioned by the police, he was found to be in possession of £100 and a false identity card.

◄ **Yardley Hastings Castle Ashby Road c1950** Y43002

Here we have another view of picturesque thatched cottages in the village. This entire area was once cloaked with trees: it was once part of a forest that extended for miles across the surrounding countryside. The village once belonged to a Saxon earl, and then to William the Conqueror's niece.

Yardley Gobion, High Street c1965 Y42005
Close to the county's southern boundary, the village of Yardley Gobion is flanked by the Grand Union Canal and the River Tove. Not long before this photograph was taken, the place consisted of the High Street and just a couple of other roads. A council estate and two private estates helped to boost the population over the years.

Yardley Gobion, Grafton Road c1965 Y42001
Older residents of Yardley Gobion will remember when this village had four pubs and five shops. There were even two bakehouses and two blacksmiths at one time, but the village community has changed a great deal since those far-off days. Around the time this picture was taken, a number of post-medieval pottery kilns were found in the village.

Northampton
Market Place and the Mobbs Memorial 1922 72168
Though no longer in the Market Place, this fine monument to
Lieutenant-Colonel Edgar Mobbs was once a famous landmark in
Northampton. Mobbs was a noted Midlands sportsman; having enlisted
as a private during the First World War, he rose through the ranks to
command his battalion. As well as bearing his bust, the monument also
depicts football and battle scenes. Crowning the pedestal is a bronze
figure carrying a torch and wreath in memory of Mobbs.

**Northampton
From All Saints'
Church Tower 1922**
72166
Sad to say, the tower
of All Saints' Church is
not safe at present, so it
is not possible to climb
to the top and compare
this photograph with
the reality of present-
day Northampton.
However, if you did go
up, you would see that
the Market Place is still
covered by stalls.

◀ **Northampton, Market Place c1950** N40008
Much of this corner of the Market Place has changed since this photograph was taken. The newspaper office on the left and the road running to the right of it have gone; in their place is a modern shopping complex. The Midland Railway Hotel on the right is also a shopping centre - Peacock Place. Three doors up is a building with a bay window on the first floor. A solicitor's office since 1949, this was once a locally famous music school.

◄ **Northampton Market Place 1922**

72169

Stand where this picture was taken, and you can see that the fountain in the middle of the square is no longer there. Many of the buildings on the left have been demolished to make way for modern shops and offices. Waterloo House has also gone, to be replaced by an office building, though the church tower is still clearly visible.

◄ **Northampton, Market Place c1950** N40010

Few buildings remain untouched by the passing of the years in this sunny picture of the Market Place. The impressive Royal Insurance building and the premises of Abel's Pianos have both gone; the Admiral Rodney pub, Household Linens, the Queen's Arms and Victoria House, at the very end of the row, have changed hands and been refurbished over the years.

Northampton
George Row 1922 72178
Just round the corner from the church is George Row. The buildings
look pretty much the same today, though Henry Cooper's film
developing business and the premises of the Midland Lace Association
have gone. With the hoods of the cars down and the trees clearly in
leaf, this photograph was obviously taken at the height of summer.

Northampton
All Saints' Church 1922 72191
Since this photograph was taken, the street has become much busier with traffic;
these days it would be difficult to stroll about without fear of being knocked down.
Note the traffic policeman and the tram lines. Much of All Saints' Church was
destroyed in a big fire in the town in 1675, though the medieval tower survives.
The clock face has changed, and the trees and the tram wires have long gone.

**Northampton
George Row 1922**
72179
On the extreme right of the picture is Northampton's County Hall headquarters. The Hall dates back to 1678, and was the first public building to be constructed after the fire of 1675. The County Hall was designed by Sir Roger Norwich, who was MP for the town. The County Court, part of the building, closed some years ago and was moved to another part of town.

Northampton
The Guildhall 1922 72181
This heavily-decorated Victorian building was built by E W Godwin
in 1864; as the picture demonstrates, it consists of two storeys
with a clock tower, a turreted gable and endless lines of windows.
Between the upper windows are pillars with standing statues under
canopies. From right to left they represent the Archangel Michael,
Edward IV, Henry VII, Queen Victoria, Edward I, Henry III, Richard I,
St George, St Andrew and St Patrick.

Northampton, The Guildhall c1955 N40023
The Archangel Michael, Northampton's patron saint, can just be seen in this photograph, crowning the Guildhall's turreted gable. The buildings to the right have made way for an extension to the Guildhall, opened in 1992. New street lamps also replace the ones in this picture, and the street was wider then than now.

Northampton, Mercers Row c1955 N40018
The splendid Westminster Bank building on the corner of Mercers Row, distinguished by its striking dome, is now a branch of Nationwide; the tall, narrow building to the right of it is a jeweller and diamond merchant. Many of the buildings to the right of it remain the same. Boots, on the left of the picture, later became the premises of a linen shop. The church's magnificent portico was completed in 1701.

Northampton Mercers Row c1950

N40001

The cars parked on the left of the picture may well be taxis. Rising above the cars is the impressive edifice of H Samuel, the famous High Street jeweller. Just visible to the left is All Saints Church. Its splendid portico, just around the corner, is a reminder of St Paul's Cathedral.

Northampton
The Drapery 1922
72174
Note the many shop
awnings and the trams
further down the street,
a reminder of town
centre public transport.

◄ **Northampton
The Drapery c1950**
N40005
This very detailed
photograph depicts one
of Northampton's busiest
streets. On the right is the
splendid facade of the old
Northamptonshire Union
Bank, which became the
National Provincial Bank
and today is Nat West.
The buildings to the right
of it remain, though the
Chamber of Commerce
sign has gone. Peeping
above the rooftops is the
dome of All Saints Church.

Northampton
The Drapery c1955
N40056

Northampton shod most of Cromwell's army; over the years it acquired status as an important boot and shoe manufacturing centre. The Drapery and Mercers Row also recall its connection with the textile industry. The traffic island has been removed since this photograph was taken.

▼ Northampton
The Hospital 1922   72183

The bust of Edward VII is still there today. The inscription beside it reads: 'Thoughtful for the care and cure of the sick, he founded the King Edward Hospital Fund and left to the world a noble example of wise philanthropy'. The memorial was unveiled in 1913. Prince Albert laid the foundation stone for the wing on the right in 1887. The lodge by the gate has now gone.

◄ Northampton
Abington Street 1922
72172

The tram lines and the traffic have long disappeared, and now Abington Street is pedestrianised. Today, most of the buildings date only from the 1960s and 1970s - the street looks better in this photograph than it does now. On the right is the Notre Dame School, founded by two sisters in the mid 19th century. The school closed in 1975, and the building was later demolished.

Northampton, Gold Street c1950 N40004
The ornately decorated Weaver to Wearer shop premises on the right is now a cafe bar; the Queen's Head pub next to it has been replaced by a modern shoe shop. Burtons has also gone, though the Victorian Grand Hotel on the opposite side of the street remains.

Northampton, The River Nene 1922 72187
The River Nene flows through Northampton; it has been an important artery through the county for centuries. One of its key roles was to provide cheap and easy transport when roads were difficult to negotiate. As a result, tanners and shoemakers set up in business along its banks.

Index

Frith Book Co Titles

www.francisfrith.co.uk

The Frith Book Company publishes over 100 new titles each year. A selection of those currently available is listed below. For latest catalogue please contact Frith Book Co.
Town Books 96 pages, approximately 100 photos. *County and Themed Books* 128 pages, approximately 150 photos (unless specified). All titles hardback with laminated case and jacket, except those indicated pb (paperback)

Amersham, Chesham & Rickmansworth (pb)	1-85937-340-2	£9.99	Derbyshire Living Memories	1-85937-330-5	£14.99
Andover (pb)	1-85937-292-9	£9.99	Devon Churches (pb)	1-85937-250-3	£9.99
Aylesbury (pb)	1-85937-227-9	£9.99	Dorchester (pb)	1-85937-307-0	£9.99
Barnstaple (pb)	1-85937-300-3	£9.99	Dorset (pb)	1-85937-269-4	£9.99
Basildon Living Memories (pb)	1-85937-515-4	£9.99	Down the Severn (pb)	1-85937-560-x	£9.99
Bath (pb)	1-85937-419-0	£9.99	Down The Thames (pb)	1-85937-278-3	£9.99
Bedford (pb)	1-85937-205-8	£9.99	Down the Trent	1-85937-311-9	£14.99
Bedfordshire Living Memories	1-85937-513-8	£14.99	East Anglia (pb)	1-85937-265-1	£9.99
Belfast (pb)	1-85937-303-8	£9.99	East Grinstead (pb)	1-85937-138-8	£9.99
Berkshire (pb)	1-85937-191-4	£9.99	East Sussex (pb)	1-85937-606-1	£9.99
Berkshire Churches	1-85937-170-1	£17.99	Eastbourne (pb)	1-85937-399-2	£9.99
Berkshire Living Memories	1-85937-332-1	£14.99	Edinburgh (pb)	1-85937-193-0	£8.99
Blackpool (pb)	1-85937-393-3	£9.99	Essex - Second Selection	1-85937-456-5	£14.99
Bognor Regis (pb)	1-85937-431-x	£9.99	Essex (pb)	1-85937-270-8	£9.99
Bournemouth (pb)	1-85937-545-6	£9.99	Essex Coast	1-85937-342-9	£14.99
Bradford (pb)	1-85937-204-x	£9.99	Essex Living Memories	1-85937-490-5	£14.99
Bridgend (pb)	1-85937-386-0	£7.99	Exeter	1-85937-539-1	£9.99
Bridgwater (pb)	1-85937-305-4	£9.99	Exmoor (pb)	1-85937-608-8	£9.99
Bridport (pb)	1-85937-327-5	£9.99	Falmouth (pb)	1-85937-594-4	£9.99
Brighton (pb)	1-85937-192-2	£8.99	Folkestone (pb)	1-85937-124-8	£9.99
Bristol (pb)	1-85937-264-3	£9.99	Frome (pb)	1-85937-317-8	£9.99
British Life A Century Ago (pb)	1-85937-213-9	£9.99	Glamorgan	1-85937-488-3	£14.99
Buckinghamshire (pb)	1-85937-200-7	£9.99	Glasgow (pb)	1-85937-190-6	£9.99
Camberley (pb)	1-85937-222-8	£9.99	Glastonbury (pb)	1-85937-338-0	£7.99
Cambridge (pb)	1-85937-422-0	£9.99	Gloucester (pb)	1-85937-232-5	£9.99
Cambridgeshire (pb)	1-85937-420-4	£9.99	Gloucestershire (pb)	1-85937-561-8	£9.99
Cambridgeshire Villages	1-85937-523-5	£14.99	Greater Manchester (pb)	1-85937-266-x	£9.99
Canals And Waterways (pb)	1-85937-291-0	£9.99	Guildford (pb)	1-85937-410-7	£9.99
Canterbury Cathedral (pb)	1-85937-179-5	£9.99	Hampshire (pb)	1-85937-279-1	£9.99
Carmarthenshire (pb)	1-85937-604-5	£9.99	Harrogate (pb)	1-85937-423-9	£9.99
Chelmsford (pb)	1-85937-310-0	£9.99	Hastings and Bexhill (pb)	1-85937-131-0	£9.99
Cheltenham (pb)	1-85937-095-0	£9.99	Heart of Lancashire (pb)	1-85937-197-3	£9.99
Cheshire (pb)	1-85937-271-6	£9.99	Helston (pb)	1-85937-214-7	£9.99
Chester (pb)	1-85937-382-8	£9.99	Hereford (pb)	1-85937-175-2	£9.99
Chesterfield (pb)	1-85937-378-x	£9.99	Herefordshire (pb)	1-85937-567-7	£9.99
Chichester (pb)	1-85937-228-7	£9.99	Herefordshire Living Memories	1-85937-514-6	£14.99
Churches of East Cornwall (pb)	1-85937-249-x	£9.99	Hertfordshire (pb)	1-85937-247-3	£9.99
Churches of Hampshire (pb)	1-85937-207-4	£9.99	Horsham (pb)	1-85937-432-8	£9.99
Cinque Ports & Two Ancient Towns	1-85937-492-1	£14.99	Humberside (pb)	1-85937-605-3	£9.99
Colchester (pb)	1-85937-188-4	£8.99	Hythe, Romney Marsh, Ashford (pb)	1-85937-256-2	£9.99
Cornwall Living Memories	1-85937-248-1	£14.99	Ipswich (pb)	1-85937-424-7	£9.99
Cotswolds (pb)	1-85937-230-9	£9.99	Isle of Man (pb)	1-85937-268-6	£9.99
Cotswolds Living Memories	1-85937-255-4	£14.99	Isle of Wight (pb)	1-85937-429-8	£9.99
County Durham (pb)	1-85937-398-4	£9.99	Isle of Wight Living Memories	1-85937-304-6	£14.99
Croydon Living Memories (pb)	1-85937-162-0	£9.99	Kent (pb)	1-85937-189-2	£9.99
Derby (pb)	1-85937-367-4	£9.99	Kent Living Memories(pb)	1-85937-401-8	£9.99
Derbyshire (pb)	1-85937-196-5	£9.99	Kings Lynn (pb)	1-85937-334-8	£9.99

Available from your local bookshop or from the publisher

Frith Book Co Titles (continued)

Title	ISBN	Price	Title	ISBN	Price
Leicester (pb)	1-85937-381-x	£9.99	Sherborne (pb)	1-85937-301-1	£9.99
Leicestershire & Rutland Living Memories	1-85937-500-6	£12.99	Shrewsbury (pb)	1-85937-325-9	£9.99
Leicestershire (pb)	1-85937-185-x	£9.99	Shropshire (pb)	1-85937-326-7	£9.99
Lighthouses	1-85937-257-0	£9.99	Shropshire Living Memories	1-85937-643-6	£14.99
Lincoln (pb)	1-85937-380-1	£9.99	South Devon Living Memories (pb)	1-85937-609-6	£9.99
Lincolnshire (pb)	1-85937-433-6	£9.99	South East London (pb)	1-85937-263-5	£9.99
Liverpool and Merseyside (pb)	1-85937-234-1	£9.99	South Somerset	1-85937-318-6	£14.99
London (pb)	1-85937-183-3	£9.99	South Wales	1-85937-519-7	£14.99
London Living Memories	1-85937-454-9	£14.99	Southampton (pb)	1-85937-427-1	£9.99
Ludlow (pb)	1-85937-176-0	£9.99	Southport (pb)	1-85937-425-5	£9.99
Luton (pb)	1-85937-235-x	£9.99	St Albans (pb)	1-85937-341-0	£9.99
Maidenhead (pb)	1-85937-339-9	£9.99	St Ives (pb)	1-85937-415-8	£9.99
Maidstone (pb)	1-85937-391-7	£9.99	Stafford Living Memories (pb)	1-85937-503-0	£9.99
Marlborough (pb)	1-85937-336-4	£9.99	Staffordshire (pb)	1-85937-308-9	£9.99
Middlesex	1-85937-158-2	£14.99	Stourbridge (pb)	1-85937-530-8	£9.99
Monmouthshire	1-85937-532-4	£14.99	Stratford upon Avon (pb)	1-85937-388-7	£9.99
New Forest (pb)	1-85937-390-9	£9.99	Suffolk (pb)	1-85937-221-x	£9.99
Newark (pb)	1-85937-366-6	£9.99	Suffolk Coast (pb)	1-85937-610-x	£9.99
Newquay (pb)	1-85937-421-2	£9.99	Surrey (pb)	1-85937-240-6	£9.99
Norfolk (pb)	1-85937-195-7	£9.99	Surrey Living Memories	1-85937-328-3	£14.99
Norfolk Broads	1-85937-486-7	£14.99	Sussex (pb)	1-85937-184-1	£9.99
Norfolk Living Memories (pb)	1-85937-402-6	£9.99	Sutton (pb)	1-85937-337-2	£9.99
North Buckinghamshire	1-85937-626-6	£14.99	Swansea (pb)	1-85937-167-1	£9.99
North Devon Living Memories	1-85937-261-9	£14.99	Taunton (pb)	1-85937-314-3	£9.99
North Hertfordshire	1-85937-547-2	£14.99	Tees Valley & Cleveland (pb)	1-85937-623-1	£9.99
North London (pb)	1-85937-403-4	£9.99	Teignmouth (pb)	1-85937-370-4	£7.99
North Somerset	1-85937-302-x	£14.99	Thanet (pb)	1-85937-116-7	£9.99
North Wales (pb)	1-85937-298-8	£9.99	Tiverton (pb)	1-85937-178-7	£9.99
North Yorkshire (pb)	1-85937-236-8	£9.99	Torbay (pb)	1-85937-597-9	£9.99
Northamptonshire Living Memories	1-85937-529-4	£14.99	Truro (pb)	1-85937-598-7	£9.99
Northamptonshire	1-85937-150-7	£14.99	Victorian & Edwardian Dorset	1-85937-254-6	£14.99
Northumberland	1-85937-522-7	£14.99	Victorian & Edwardian Kent (pb)	1-85937-624-X	£9.99
Norwich (pb)	1-85937-194-9	£8.99	Victorian & Edwardian Maritime Album (pb)	1-85937-622-3	£9.99
Nottingham (pb)	1-85937-324-0	£9.99	Victorian and Edwardian Sussex (pb)	1-85937-625-8	£9.99
Nottinghamshire (pb)	1-85937-187-6	£9.99	Villages of Devon (pb)	1-85937-293-7	£9.99
Oxford (pb)	1-85937-411-5	£9.99	Villages of Kent (pb)	1-85937-294-5	£9.99
Oxfordshire (pb)	1-85937-430-1	£9.99	Warrington (pb)	1-85937-507-3	£9.99
Oxfordshire Living Memories	1-85937-525-1	£14.99	Warwick (pb)	1-85937-518-9	£9.99
Paignton (pb)	1-85937-374-7	£7.99	Welsh Castles (pb)	1-85937-322-4	£9.99
Peak District (pb)	1-85937-280-5	£9.99	West Yorkshire (pb)	1-85937-201-5	£9.99
Penzance (pb)	1-85937-595-2	£9.99	Weymouth (pb)	1-85937-209-0	£9.99
Peterborough (pb)	1-85937-219-8	£9.99	Wiltshire (pb)	1-85937-277-5	£9.99
Picturesque Harbours	1-85937-208-2	£14.99	Wiltshire Churches (pb)	1-85937-171-x	£9.99
Piers	1-85937-237-6	£17.99	Wiltshire Living Memories (pb)	1-85937-396-8	£9.99
Plymouth (pb)	1-85937-389-5	£9.99	Winchester (pb)	1-85937-428-x	£9.99
Poole & Sandbanks (pb)	1-85937-251-1	£9.99	Windsor (pb)	1-85937-333-x	£9.99
Redhill to Reigate (pb)	1-85937-596-0	£9.99	Wokingham & Bracknell (pb)	1-85937-329-1	£9.99
Ringwood (pb)	1-85937-384-4	£7.99	Woodbridge (pb)	1-85937-498-0	£9.99
Romford (pb)	1-85937-319-4	£9.99	Worcester (pb)	1-85937-165-5	£9.99
Royal Tunbridge Wells (pb)	1-85937-504-9	£9.99	York (pb)	1-85937-199-x	£9.99
Salisbury (pb)	1-85937-239-2	£9.99	Yorkshire (pb)	1-85937-186-8	£9.99
Scarborough (pb)	1-85937-379-8	£9.99	Yorkshire Coastal Memories	1-85937-506-5	£14.99
Sevenoaks and Tonbridge (pb)	1-85937-392-5	£9.99	Yorkshire Dales	1-85937-502-2	£14.99

See Frith books on the internet at www.francisfrith.co.uk

FRITH PRODUCTS & SERVICES

Francis Frith would doubtless be pleased to know that the pioneering publishing venture he started in 1860 still continues today. Over a hundred and forty years later, The Francis Frith Collection continues in the same innovative tradition and is now one of the foremost publishers of vintage photographs in the world. Some of the current activities include:

Interior Decoration

Today Frith's photographs can be seen framed and as giant wall murals in thousands of pubs, restaurants, hotels, banks, retail stores and other public buildings throughout the country. In every case they enhance the unique local atmosphere of the places they depict and provide reminders of gentler days in an increasingly busy and frenetic world.

Product Promotions

Frith products are used by many major companies to promote the sales of their own products or to reinforce their own history and heritage. Frith promotions have been used by Hovis bread, Courage beers, Scots Porage Oats, Colman's mustard, Cadbury's foods, Mellow Birds coffee, Dunhill pipe tobacco, Guinness, and Bulmer's Cider.

Genealogy and Family History

As the interest in family history and roots grows world-wide, more and more people are turning to Frith's photographs of Great Britain for images of the towns, villages and streets where their ancestors lived; and, of course, photographs of the churches and chapels where their ancestors were christened, married and buried are an essential part of every genealogy tree and family album.

Frith Products

All Frith photographs are available Framed or just as Mounted Prints and Posters (size 23 x 16 inches). These may be ordered from the address below. From time to time other products - Address Books, Maps, etc - are available.

The Internet

Already fifty thousand Frith photographs can be viewed and purchased on the internet through the Frith websites and a myriad of partner sites.

For more detailed information on Frith companies and products, look at these sites:

www.francisfrith.co.uk
www.francisfrith.com
(for North American visitors)

See the complete list of Frith Books at:
www.francisfrith.co.uk
This web site is regularly updated with the latest list of publications from the Frith Book Company. If you wish to buy books relating to another part of the country that your local bookshop does not stock, you may purchase on-line.

For further information, trade, or author enquiries please contact us at the address below:
The Francis Frith Collection, Frith's Barn, Teffont, Salisbury, Wiltshire, England SP3 5QP.
Tel: +44 (0)1722 716 376 Fax: +44 (0)1722 716 881   Email: sales@francisfrith.co.uk

See Frith books on the internet at www.francisfrith.co.uk

FREE PRINT OF YOUR CHOICE

Mounted Print
Overall size 14 x 11 inches (355 x 280mm)

Choose any Frith photograph in this book.
Simply complete the Voucher opposite and return it with your remittance for £2.25 (to cover postage and handling) and we will print the photograph of your choice in SEPIA (size 11 x 8 inches) and supply it in a cream mount with a burgundy rule line (overall size 14 x 11 inches).
Please note: photographs with a reference number starting with a "Z" are not Frith photographs and cannot be supplied under this offer.
Offer valid for delivery to one UK address only.

PLUS: **Order additional Mounted Prints at HALF PRICE - £7.49 each** (normally £14.99)
If you would like to order more Frith prints from this book, possibly as gifts for friends and family, you can buy them at half price (with no additional postage and handling costs).

PLUS: **Have your Mounted Prints framed**
For an extra £14.95 per print you can have your mounted print(s) framed in an elegant polished wood and gilt moulding, overall size 16 x 13 inches (no additional postage and handling required).

IMPORTANT!

These special prices are only available if you use this form to order . You must use the ORIGINAL VOUCHER on this page (no copies permitted). We can only despatch to one UK address. This offer cannot be combined with any other offer.

Send completed Voucher form to:
The Francis Frith Collection, Frith's Barn, Teffont, Salisbury, Wiltshire SP3 5QP

CHOOSE A PHOTOGRAPH FROM THIS BOOK

Voucher for **FREE** and Reduced Price Frith Prints

Please do not photocopy this voucher. Only the original is valid, so please fill it in, cut it out and return it to us with your order.

Picture ref no	Page no	Qty	Mounted @ £7.49	Framed + £14.95	Total Cost £
		1	Free of charge*	£	£
			£7.49	£	£
			£7.49	£	£
			£7.49	£	£
			£7.49	£	£
			£7.49	£	£
Please allow 28 days for delivery. Offer available to one UK address only			* Post & handling		£2.25
			Total Order Cost		£

Title of this book . . . .
I enclose a cheque/postal order for £ . . . .
made payable to 'The Francis Frith Collection'

OR please debit my Mastercard / Visa / Maestro / Amex card, details below

Card Number

Issue No (Maestro only)   Valid from (Maestro)

Expires   Signature

Name Mr/Mrs/Ms . . . .
Address . . . .
. . . .
. . . .
. . . . Postcode . . . .
Daytime Tel No . . . .
Email . . . .

Valid to 31/12/07

Would you like to find out more about Francis Frith?

We have recently recruited some entertaining speakers who are happy to visit local groups, clubs and societies to give an illustrated talk documenting Frith's travels and photographs. If you are a member of such a group and are interested in hosting a presentation, we would love to hear from you.

Our speakers bring with them a small selection of our local town and county books, together with sample prints. They are happy to take orders. A small proportion of the order value is donated to the group who have hosted the presentation. The talks are therefore an excellent way of fundraising for small groups and societies.

Can you help us with information about any of the Frith photographs in this book?

We are gradually compiling an historical record for each of the photographs in the Frith archive. It is always fascinating to find out the names of the people shown in the pictures, as well as insights into the shops, buildings and other features depicted.

If you recognize anyone in the photographs in this book, or if you have information not already included in the author's caption, do let us know. We would love to hear from you, and will try to publish it in future books or articles.

Our production team

Frith books are produced by a small dedicated team at offices in the converted Grade II listed 18th-century barn at Teffont near Salisbury, illustrated above. Most have worked with the Frith Collection for many years. All have in common one quality: they have a passion for the Frith Collection. The team is constantly expanding, but currently includes:

Paul Baron, Phillip Brennan, Jason Buck, John Buck, Ruth Butler, Heather Crisp, David Davies, Louis du Mont, Isobel Hall, Gareth Harris, Lucy Hart, Julian Hight, Peter Horne, James Kinnear, Karen Kinnear, Tina Leary, Stuart Login, David Marsh, Lesley-Ann Millard, Sue Molloy, Glenda Morgan, Wayne Morgan, Sarah Roberts, Kate Rotondetto, Dean Scource, Eliza Sackett, Terence Sackett, Sandra Sampson, Adrian Sanders, Sandra Sanger, Jan Scrivens, Julia Skinner, David Smith, Miles Smith, Lewis Taylor, Shelley Tolcher, Lorraine Tuck, Amanita Wainwright and Ricky Williams.

Free Print – see overleaf